TELL ME THE TRUTH

a code for freedom

Olga Sheean

InsideOut Media

For a free download of the poster that accompanies this book, go to https://olgasheean.com/tell-me

Olga Sheean also offers consultations and courses to help people embody the deeper truth in their lives and to explore their own empowerment.

For details, visit https://olgasheean.com

Details of other books by Olga Sheean are included at the end of this book and can be found at https://olgasheean.com/books

ISBN: 978-1-928103-12-7 (e-book)

978-1-928103-13-4 (printed book)

Published by InsideOut Media: info@insideoutmedia.net

Cover image: PublicCo on Pixabay.com

Cover design and layout: Lewis Evans (lewisevans.net)

The truth is simple.

It's the lies that complicate things.

INTRODUCTION

We stand at a crucial crossroads in our evolution. In one direction lies the superhighway of technology—a spaghetti junction of wireless gadgetry and never-ending techno-evolution. As we race along this route, seduced by a futuristic lifestyle, we keep ourselves distracted from the deeper truth. The truth about this technology is not quite as life-enhancing as we might think (although the deeper truth about *us* is everything we could wish for). The truth is that we are surrendering our humanity to inanimate devices, undermining our viability as a species.

The alternative route—the scenic route—seems less appealing, as we are so used to fast living and non-stop mental stimulation. This is the road of consciousness and spiritual evolution—the most powerful yet most neglected aspect of our existence. In this direction lie freedom and fulfillment, although it may not look like that when standing at the crossroads.

Unless we change direction in favour of human evolution, the materialism of our techno-times will inevitably cancel out the very essence of our humanness. Our lives will be run by machines; artificial intelligence will manipulate our world; our bodies will be overwhelmed by electrical stimuli and wireless radiation; and we will have no control over industry or governments.

Do you like being a human database?

In choosing technology over humanity, we are losing our human functionality in two vital ways: 1) as more and more of our functions are taken over by machines and gadgets, we ourselves become a commodity—a source of data to be exploited by commercial interests; and 2) we are suffering increasing functional impairment, due to gadget-driven living and the adverse biological effects of wireless radiation.

We used to be consumers, hungry for information and success. Now, we are being consumed, one gadget and one sales pitch at a time. Our humanity is slipping through our fingers, with more texting than touching, more head than heart, and more screen time than face time.

Human consciousness is really all we have. If we trade that for inanimate technology, we defeat the very purpose of our existence. We forget that we are here to evolve, to fully experience our multi-faceted selves, and to achieve fulfillment, happiness, self-mastery and peace.

In this world of techno-wizardry, we are not being treated as precious human beings with our own delicate electrical systems, inevitably affected by invasive manmade electromagnetic fields. We are merely part of a massive commercial machine that cares only for our commercial value. We are also distracted by all the gadgetry, which deflects our attention from the deeper internal processes that are actually creating the symptoms of disease and dysfunction in our bodies and on our planet.

This book is your antidote to the tsunami of commercial spin, external stimuli and bad news clogging our news channels and our consciousness. It challenges you to remember who you are and to change direction in favour of humanity and life. See the spin for what it is; let go of over-stimulation so you can reconnect with the real you; and trade the bad news for the good news and the truth about you and your world.

Bad news and commercial spin promote fear and distort the truth. They cause us to forget who we are. They misrepresent our reality and disregard our creative capacity for change. Sharing bad news gives it power, while diminishing our awareness of our own power to live a superlative life.

It distorts our sense of self, keeping us contained in a state of anxiety and trepidation. Caught up in the challenges of fast-paced living and sensory overload, many of us have forgotten what we are capable of …if we ever knew.

Sharing the good news (the truth) and focusing on the positive things in life—especially our phenomenal spiritual and creative faculties—elevates us to a higher plane of possibilities where we realize that we can have and be so much more, when we let go of external props and distractions.

The bad news has nothing to do with who we truly are, although it shows us what happens when we lose our way. The deeper truth is something else altogether. When we embrace it, we unhook from the world of grasping consumerism and discover a far more compelling reality. When we embody it, we find freedom. And what is freedom if not the ability to think, feel, do and be what we choose? To be who we want to be and who we really are: *that* is conscious evolution—the only kind of evolution worth living for.

I am telling you the truth.

Now it's your turn.

The most important truth
is the truth you tell yourself,
because it defines your existence.

How to use this book

In reading this book, imagine that I am talking to the ultimate you—*the you* that would emerge if you could shed your limiting beliefs, drop all the distractions and be your true self. In this state, you would see the power of you—what you are capable of doing and achieving when you are not constrained by convention, inhibited by fears/self-doubts, or disconnected from your innate co-creative capacities.

This is *the you* that can create a rich and rewarding life, inspired to fulfill your dreams and be your very best self.

When you are fully you, you are in charge of your mind, you are in touch with your body, you are connected to your true essence, and you can harness the power of all three in orchestrating a life that you love.

Whatever is happening in your life, it is all about you. You are the agent of change and the magnet that attracts whatever reality you subconsciously believe you deserve and whatever growth needs to happen for you to fulfill your potential.

In the following pages, you will get a sense of what has been missing for you, why it matters and how to get it back. You will find yourself asking some deeper questions and reflecting on your choices. You will be re-united with the deeper truth about you and what it means to be fully human. You will find out how to thrive as an enlightened, autonomous individual with a quest for personal excellence and fulfillment.

Remember who you really are and why you are here.

Remember that you are powerful, with the capacity to orchestrate your life and influence your world.

Remember that you can choose a higher path and that only the deeper truth about you will set you free to be all that you can be.

I.
Give me the good news first
...and last and in between.

There is a vast and wondrous world of good news that few people ever access because they don't realize that it exists. It contains a deeper truth about everything that happens, giving us a profound new understanding of how our reality works, beyond what we see with our eyes, touch with our hands or hear on the news.

There is also the bad news and it's easy to get lost in it. If we give it airtime, we can become overwhelmed and emotionally numbed by it. We can lose touch with our sense of joy and possibility, and what we are capable of, as individuals.

Bad news seems like bad news because we think we cannot do anything about it. We see circumstances as being beyond our control and we must simply do the best we can to deal with them. The good news is that everything that happens in our life is a reflection of what is going on inside us. It is a physical manifestation of the power of our beliefs and emotions to shape our lives—our relationships, our challenges, our health concerns, our careers, our choices.

The good news about that good news is that we therefore have the power to change our circumstances. We are not at the mercy of circumstances (unless we choose to be) and we do have the capacity to access the deeper truth about ourselves and to make sense of our seemingly chaotic world.

We must stop defending the lies
that prevent us from becoming
the powerful person we are designed to be.

Change your mind, change your life

You may find yourself doubting these concepts. Do you need proof that you are powerful? Do you want hard evidence of your capacity to create what you really want? You might, if you have been deeply programmed to not trust yourself or to perceive the world as a tough, unfriendly place. But needing proof puts you in the position of building a case against yourself. It's like challenging a jury to prove that you are powerless until proven to be powerful.

Let go of the need for proof so that there is space for something else to come in. Learn to trust in the power of you, and remember that you can only practise trust in the face of uncertainty. If you know everything, you don't need to trust, yet trusting in the power of you is exactly what you must do if you want to be free to live your ultimate life.

It's easier and a lot more fun to just accept the truth and run with it. Make it work for you. Prove to yourself that it is true—by applying the principles and witnessing the results. A clever concept might bring some temporary relief if it provides you with a kinder, more optimistic perspective of yourself, but it's really only useful if it's applied in practical ways in your everyday life.

The good news—and the basis for all future good news—is that you are powerful. You have all the faculties you need to transform your circumstances and find true fulfillment.

The first step towards that transformation involves accepting that truth about you and choosing to focus exclusively on the good news, inside and out, knowing that you play a pivotal role in leveraging its impact.

Don't feed the bad news—whether it's about something political or something personal in your own life.

Don't feed any negative stories—about yourself, your partner or anyone else.

Don't get caught up in the commercial spin on your life; you are a precious resource, not a data-rich commodity to be sold online. You are a valuable human being, with a beating heart, profound emotions and talents that have the power to change your world.

Remember who you really are. Share the deeper truth and your good news—and watch both expand in the sharing, lifting your mood and transmitting a positive vibe. Put a positive spin on everything, no matter how contrived or corny it feels. Praise yourself for things well done (and let the other stuff fade into the background).

Be a beacon of light and positivity, and you will see things start to change around you. You will become a magnet for more of the same.

Leverage your magnetism

Every thought has an electrical charge. Every emotion has magnetism. Together, these two things define your mood, your personality and your presence, transmitting a very specific electromagnetic message or 'story' about who you believe yourself to be, what you think you are worth and how powerful you are.

What you transmit defines your reality, one thought and one emotion at a time. Transmit good news, positive vibes and uplifting energy, and good things will come to you in myriad ways that could not have been orchestrated by your mind or hard work alone.

Good news breeds more good news. It's every bit as infectious as bad news, but a whole lot healthier and far more rewarding.

Sharing and focusing on the good in your life (whether it's

your good health, the birds singing in your garden or a smile from the postman), while screening out all negativity (whether it's negative friends or the news on TV) tells the universe that you expect good things, that you are a recipient for good things, and that you deserve good things. And good things you will get, if you embody the truth about you and leverage the power of your own electromagnetism in co-creation with universal wisdom.

2.
Don't tell me how doomed our world is or what you feel it owes you.

I want to hear about the power of you.

When we talk about our challenges or problems, we are actually telling two stories: one that relates to our physical circumstances, and one that lies beneath our words. We might think we are just telling someone about a problem at work or an issue with a partner, but once we understand that our circumstances are a direct result of our beliefs (and the thoughts and actions that result), we realize that we are telling them something else entirely. If we talk about being criticized or disrespected, for example, we are inadvertently telling people that we are not deserving of respect, since this is what we have attracted ...and we always attract a reflection of what we subconsciously believe about ourselves.

The circumstances of your life tell the story that you were told about you, in your formative years. Buried in your subconscious, there are numerous programs that determine what you think, how you feel, what you say and how you behave. Many of those programs are positive, keeping you safe or giving you a strong sense of right and wrong. However, there are many negative programs also, and they are the ones that make life unnecessarily challenging, cramping your style and preventing you from finding joy, peace and your inner power. Yet they are also your pathway to deeper understanding and to the ultimate mastery of self, once you know how to work with them.

If *the empowered you* were telling me about the power of you, you would tell me a very different story. Instead of telling me that you hate the way your boss treats you and that you're looking for another job, for example, you might say that you can see how your boss triggers feelings of inadequacy and not being good enough. You would tell me that you are consciously working to transform those feelings into their healthy opposites: competence, confidence and a deep sense of being more than good enough. You would realize that you have never really felt confident or good enough, and that those feelings have nothing to do with your boss. You would tell me that you are now striving to embody and demonstrate those missing qualities so that they eventually become a natural part of you, transmitting a very different message about your value, commanding more respect and generating greater success and rewards than ever before.

In acknowledging your power to attract or generate certain scenarios in your life, you take ownership and responsibility for your feelings and reactions, rather than blaming them on someone else or some outside force that appears to have nothing to do with you.

Yet what happens in your life has everything to do with you. The power of you guarantees that it be so, because you are that powerful.

The truth has power
and the power of the truth
is the power of you

3.
Tell me what magic you created in your world today.

Magic happens in your life when you activate your full self, when you tap into your co-creative powers and when you start to use your mind to consciously manifest what you desire. It could take the form of an unexpected windfall, a seemingly spontaneous recovery from disease, the appearance of your ideal loving partner, or whatever else you have been envisioning.

We are usually so focused on our external world that we give little time to what is going on inside ...unless our body starts to give us messages about self-neglect or tells us that we are off track with our purpose. The fact that we get ill and often have physical symptoms (whether it's just a headache or something more serious) reminds us that our mental, emotional, spiritual and physical selves are all interconnected. They depend on each other for balance, yet few of us manage to achieve or maintain a healthy balance in our lives, with so many stressors distracting us from what's going on at a more subtle level.

If our lives are so full of stress that we cannot make or maintain that connection, that's indication enough that we are off track. Life is not meant to be hard. Only our negative conditioning creates the challenges that we experience in our lives.

If we transform our negative beliefs into positive beliefs that acknowledge and promote our personal power, things start to flow and life becomes a whole lot easier. Becoming whole by embodying whatever qualities we failed to have cultivated in us when we were young (such as healthy self-acceptance, self-expression, validation and support), brings us the fullness of life we have been missing. When we are whole—embodying, demonstrating and expressing all of the positive qualities that we wish to see in others—we automatically attract more of the same.

It's important to remember that we are always magnetic and always transmitting positive or negative electromagnetic signals into our world. Those signals will cause us to attract positive or negative circumstances in accordance with the beliefs and emotions that we are transmitting.

When life is easy, as it is meant to be, things work like magic.

If **the enlightened you** were telling me what magic you created in your world today, you might talk to me about a breakthrough you had with a family member—someone who had alienated themselves from you for a long time, perhaps, or who consistently triggered anger/frustration/resentment every time you spoke to them. You might tell me how you diligently worked to change your own old patterns, to respond calmly and lovingly every time you were emotionally triggered, and to transform the negative 'labels' that you had subconsciously given to that person (selfish, domineering, closed) and to yourself (not heard, unappreciated, rejected). You would take pleasure in telling me how mentally changing those labels for that other person (kind, accepting, open) and for yourself (heard, appreciated, accepted) completely transformed your relationship with them.

If you were telling me what magic you created in your world today, you might tell me about the fabulous house you manifested—a house that you had been envisioning for the past year but never thought you could afford to buy. You might talk to me about the elderly man who seemingly appeared out of nowhere to tell you about this old house that he wanted to sell as quickly as possible, as he had no family and was going to live in a retirement home. You might marvel at the fact that he was asking far less than the market value and just wanted the house to go to someone who would love it, as he did for over 50 years. You might tell me that your bank manager had refused to give you a mortgage, but that your boss had stepped in and offered you one for the first five years—at the same rate of interest as the bank, with no other strings attached.

You might share with me some of the smaller breakthroughs that you might have missed before you became aware of how things worked, yet they were magic nonetheless.

You would tell me all this with a sense of wonder, because you know how things were before you began the process of changing your mind, re-writing your personal story, cultivating peace and receptivity through meditation, and choosing to believe in the power of you.

The more magic you create, the more magic you create. Using the power of your mind and spirit to manifest the things you have always wanted is an intoxicating, delightful feeling. It is like falling in love, uplifting your heart and soul, infusing you with effervescent happiness, and bringing you a profound awareness of the limitless possibilities that await those who dare to reject their old story and write a completely new one.

If we are living a lie,
we will never experience the magic
that our true selves can create

4.
Tell me what you are capable of, as a miraculous stand-alone unit of self-sufficiency, without any techno-wizardry to make you look good.

How much do you depend on gadgets, appliances or electronic devices to facilitate your life?

Think of the many devices you use. What do they add to your life ...and what do they take away?

Some appliances (such as a washing machine) make life easier and enable us to devote our time, skills and energies to more worthwhile things. Many devices that used to be manually operated (such as coffee grinders, lawnmowers and meat mincers) provided a healthy workout for our brains and bodies and promoted strong hand–eye coordination, unlike the electric, motorized or electronic versions that have replaced them. Reading a paper map, for example, has been largely replaced by GPS, preventing our brains from exercising an innate faculty linked to our survival—finding our way around, tapping into our sense of direction, and using our visual and other senses to determine where we are.

Most of us would be lost without our computers as they not only connect us to a world of information, people and opportunities, but also enable us to write, edit, design and create things in ways that would never otherwise be possible. When we use them wisely, hard-wiring them so that we have internet access without any of the downsides of wireless radiation, they can truly be a lifeline.

Other devices, such as a cell phone, can sometimes enslave us, creating a need to constantly check for messages and to respond to them straight away. Initially, having a cell phone can make us feel good, giving us a sense of importance and connectedness with others. It can even engender a sense of purpose—a sense of being active and engaged.

But what does this kind of ongoing engagement (or enslavement) say about us? We have unmet emotional needs that compel us to do things we would not otherwise do.

Why does it feel so good? Because we are desperate for acceptance, recognition, importance and a sense of belonging.

How does it affect our personal relationships? In every conceivable way, preventing us from being present and disconnecting us from our hearts.

And what about our brain, overtaxed with multi-tasking and rarely getting the chance to relax or switch off during the day, while being flooded with the feel-good dopamine that's released every time we get a message/text/e-mail/like/share?

A handy distraction

The seductive quality of wireless technology is undeniable—particularly if we want an escape from what is going on in our own lives. While the harmful radiation transmitted by wireless devices is reason enough not to use them, there are other significant downsides to our dependence …and the deep unmet needs that drive it.

Who are you with your cell phone?

Who are you without it?

What would happen to you if you lost your phone or if all the cell towers crashed and you could no longer connect?

Many people would experience extreme distress, anger and even withdrawal symptoms. A cell phone can become such an integral part of life that it can feel like an extension of one's body. For some people, being without it can feel like losing an arm.

Ironically, cell phones do many of the things that we could (and used to) do with our minds and brains if we activated them to their fullest potential. We have the capacity to communicate telepathically. When we engage our spiritual capacities, we can transmit messages and emotions to people on the other side of the world. We can connect with universal intelligence and tap into more possibilities than we could ever find through our phones.

Dependence on a cell phone distracts us from our greatness, ensuring that we remain ensnared in a web of virtual connectedness that seems to feed our deep need for love and a sense of belonging, even though a cell phone will never meet that need in a healthy, lasting way.

It's your call...

If we carry a cell phone on our person, checking it regularly, it prevents us from being present. And, if we are not present, we cannot be powerful. Only when we are in the present moment, fully conscious of what is going on inside and out, can we access the deeper connection that makes life meaningful. We cannot be truly present with a loved one if we are married to our phone.

We cannot be present for our children if we—and they—are constantly using a cell phone. Being on the phone takes us out of the moment and puts us somewhere else—in some virtual place that might provide information and/or entertainment but will not feed our souls, enable us to grow in intimacy, or cultivate a sense of peace.

But your phone does carry a very important message for you: whatever feelings or sense of loss you experience if it is taken away from you are things that you were missing before you got your phone.

For many people—people who are missing an emotional connection, a sense of purpose or belonging—this is why having a cell phone feels so good. It's not just because it's handy or because it makes them feel physically safer. It gives them the illusion of having what they feel has been missing in their lives, even though it doesn't actually change or upgrade them as a person. It doesn't give them an innate sense of connectedness with their world. It doesn't transform them into a person with healthy self-worth and self-confidence.

If **the autonomous you** were telling me what you were capable of, as a miraculous, stand-alone unit of self-sufficiency, you might tell me of the freedom you feel in letting go of gadgets—especially your cell phone. You might say that you never realized how much of you was channelled into your phone and away from the life around you.

You might tell me how much more relaxed, present and focused you feel, how your relationships have improved, how you've reconnected with your kids, and how much more peaceful your brain and body feel.

You might talk to me of the joy of cooking, of making things with your hands, of gardening, of having conversations at mealtimes, of taking the dog for a walk, of chatting to neighbours, and of reconnecting with nature and the simple things in life.

You might share with me that you used to feel uncomfortable having a meal in a restaurant on your own, and that your phone gave you something to do and made you feel less like a sorry single person sitting there alone. Now that you're more aware of this insecurity, without your phone, you're exploring it more consciously. Sometimes you read a book or you end up talking to the waiters, who appreciate diners making eye contact with them and treating them like human beings, rather than staying glued to their phone even as they place their order.

If you were telling me what you were capable of, on your own, unplugged, you might tell me that you have plugged into the power of you. You might share with me your vision of a better future and how you meditate, sitting in stillness and silence as you feed that future reality. With less focus on the outside (on your gadgets) and more on your subtle, inner feelings, you might tell me how your sleep has improved, how much more creative your brain has become, problem-solving overnight, and how much more alive and connected you feel to others than you did when you sent 50 texts and made 30 calls a day on your phone.

You might tell me that your memory is better and your brain feels sharper since you no longer rush to Google for answers to all your questions.

If you were telling me how you feel—without your electronic props, your smart appliances, your Bluetooth headset or the 1001 apps that organize your life, check your pulse and tell you what to eat—you might say that you feel happy. You might say that you feel liberated, as if you've been freed from relentless expectations and a stranglehold over every aspect of your daily life.

You might say that you are thinking for yourself, making proactive choices and exploring the deeper parts of you that technology will never reach.

You might tell me that you feel human again, without ever before realizing what that meant.

5.

Tell me how you give back to the planet that gives you life—nourishing, sheltering, supporting and inspiring you.

It can be distressing to see how our natural environment has been degraded over the decades. It reflects the way we treat our own bodies and it bears many of our emotional scars. But there is still a lot of natural beauty left and, like our bodies, nature can bounce back if we love and nurture it in the right ways …before too much damage has been done.

If *the wise you* were telling me how you give back to the planet that sustains you, you might talk to me about your organic garden and the things you grow to promote healthy soil, lots of insects, birdlife and natural pest control. You might tell me that you plant trees every year—in your own garden and as part of a community project to re-green your local environment.

You might talk of taking time to commune with nature, to get grounded on the earth, to walk in the forest or swim in the ocean, and to remember how inseparable you are from your natural world. You might tell me of the things you do to reduce the burden of waste, depletion and damage to Mother Earth:

- using only biodegradable products
- fixing anything that can be fixed, rather than throwing it away
- buying foods in bulk or loose so that no packaging is required
- re-using whatever packaging you already have
- always taking your own re-usable cotton/nylon bags with you when you shop

- buying local produce at organic farmers' markets
- eating foods that support your health and well-being
- not supporting companies that deplete or dump toxins into the environment
- disposing of/composting as much of your own waste as you possibly can
- using innovative eco-friendly forms of energy and fuel
- using as many manually operated devices/appliances as you can
- taking care of your own health, given how that also benefits the planet
- staying fit and active, since that reduces your reliance on medication/resources
- biking or walking instead of driving your car
- recycling/donating your unwanted clothing
- buying as many recycled products as possible
- not using wireless devices, to avoid harming wildlife, plants, insects, the climate, yourself and others.

You might tell me of the time you spend with others, cultivating a sense of community, sharing your experiences, expertise and wisdom, and inspiring others with the passion that you feel for biodynamic farming, nature and our planet.

You might talk to me about your gratitude—for the air you breathe, the water you drink, the beaches you walk along, the sunsets you admire and the spiritual nourishment you get from all of those things and more.

You might tell me how profoundly contented and connected you feel when you are close to nature, and how much you value this precious, irreplaceable resource in your life.

6.
Don't talk to me about our broken healthcare systems.
Tell me of your dedication to self-care.

Tell me how you nurture body, mind and planet so that none will take you prematurely home.

As miraculous walking, talking units of self-sufficiency, we have all that we need to function perfectly and to leverage our infinite creative and spiritual capacities so that we can thrive in this world. Taking care of our bodies is the most fundamental part of being human and we each have a responsibility to heed our body's needs, messages and guidance.

When we take care of our physical body, keeping it nourished, clean and clear, it provides a powerful medium for self-expression and a solid platform for launching ourselves into other dimensions. It enables us to cleanly connect with our higher selves—our soul, universal intelligence, god or whatever you perceive that life force or energy to be. It enables us to express our unique gifts and capacities in furthering the evolution of humanity and becoming all that we can be. And it enables us to experience the true happiness that comes from having a vibrantly healthy body, mind and spirit.

Not taking care of our bodies keeps us from connecting with our inner power—and it can sometimes be a subconscious way of not being proactively powerful in our lives. If we fail to take care of our own bodies, we surrender responsibility to outside forces that are unlikely to understand us, have compassion for us or heal us from dis-eases due to our disconnection from our bodies' needs and messages. Having surrendered responsibility for our well-being, we can then blame others if we are unwell—and we will have a very justifiable excuse for not moving forward with our lives in a meaningful way ...if that is something we are subconsciously afraid of doing.

If *the self-aware you* were telling me about your dedication to self-care, you might tell me you realize that taking care of your health means so much more than eating properly and exercising. You might tell me that your body is your own personal medium for evolution—a multi-dimensional, multi-faceted, profoundly complex system that interacts in ways and with realities far beyond your conscious awareness.

You might tell me that you understand how the current healthcare systems and conventional medicine ultimately put you back in charge of your own well-being, since external systems and drug-based approaches only take you further away from yourself and your own answers.

If you were telling me how you nurture your body, mind and planet, you might say that you are grateful for your own innate healing powers and for the capacity to go far beyond the limits of your physical body to connect with the universal intelligence that holds whatever deeper answers and support you might need.

You might tell me of your commitment to being fully informed about how your body works and what its symptoms represent.

You might tell me that you research what the mind can do and how you can positively re-wire your brain to change your reality and bring you more of what you want in life.

You might say you know how the choices you make in favour of your body and your spiritual health are the same choices required for sustaining a healthy planet.

7.

Tell me you can see beyond your symptoms to the messages they hold, and to your wondrous capacity to heal, regenerate your cells and change your genetic destiny.

If you were telling me what you see, beyond your physical symptoms, **the enlightened you** might share with me that your body's messages have become like a road map and even a moral compass for your life. You might tell me how your body is always guiding you towards what's best for you, and that you just have to listen.

You might share the experiences you have had in listening to your body's subtle messages and trusting your gut instincts ...and where that has taken you—perhaps to a meaningful connection with someone new, perhaps into a new relationship, perhaps to a job interview that launched you in a new direction in your life.

You might share with me your thoughts about the broader symptoms of our sickening society, and what those symptoms represent. You might say that these steadily worsening symptoms—in the form of epidemics, lifestyle diseases, social dysfunction, mental illness, addiction, dependence on pharmaceutical drugs, toxicity in our foods, erratic weather and an irradiated environment—are the result of us denying our humanness in favour of so-called economic progress, of us having surrendered our autonomy over our own bodies and minds, and of our failure to recognize our own greatness buried deep inside.

You might tell me that we are living in delusion. While we focus on each of these separate issues, bemoaning the problem, blaming governments and politicians for it, and calling for some kind of external solution, we are missing the bigger picture. These symptoms, you might say, are not meant to be addressed in isolation—and cannot be addressed unless we understand their true underlying cause.

As they grow in their severity, building to a crescendo of chaotic complexity that defies all attempts to resolve them in practical ways, these symptoms are pushing us to recognize their true source and to find a more enlightened solution. The source of these symptoms is our own internal dysfunction, and the solution lies in our own personal enlightenment. When we own the problem, you tell me, rather than blaming someone else, we can also own the solution and take responsibility for the symptoms we are all creating.

You might tell me that you have delved into the hidden realms of your subconscious mind, exploring the neural networks that shape your current existence, and how you can use your thoughts, your emotions and your intentions to feed your impassioned vision of your ideal future and make it a reality now.

You might say that you are learning to work with the energy systems of your body so you can boost your circulation, defuse stress, release blockages and revitalize yourself. You know that your body is all energy, charged by electrical impulses that are essential to your existence.

You might tell me that you can sense this energy and the energy in the world around you. With this awareness, you can tap into the greater consciousness to heal your body and regenerate your cells. You are beginning to see how you can also dissolve the beliefs or perceptions that prevent you from orchestrating your own life and influencing your own genetic destiny.

We can only know ourselves when
we uncover the deeper truth inside.

8.

Tell me how you express your love for others, why you value your own integrity, and how your humanity keeps you connected to what matters most.

If *the self-accepting you* were telling me how you express your love for others, you might tell me you realize that loving them means loving you, and loving you means loving them.

You might tell me that you have confronted your own demons and learned how to love yourself, now putting your own needs first, in healthy, everyday ways—even though you were not brought up to do so and even though some might think this selfish.

You might tell me that healthy self-love and self-acceptance are the pathways to abundance, true love and personal fulfillment, acting like magnets for more of the same.

You might share with me your commitment to being profoundly honest with those in your life, ensuring that your actions and interactions are in alignment with your values and that your thoughts, words and actions reflect your deepest, truest self.

You might tell me you are only interested in the deeper truth about yourself and others, knowing that this is the route to true intimacy and fulfillment.

You might say that you choose your relationships, your friendships and your work based on what feels right and healthy for you, always guided by your intuitive sense of where your super-conscious self is trying to take you.

If you were to talk to me about your humanity, you might say that it is your most precious faculty—the part of you that gives meaning to your life, enabling you to feel deeply, to have compassion, to have a conscience and to live mindfully, knowing that your thoughts and feelings count.

You might tell me that, in keeping you connected to what matters most, your humanity is your moral compass, guiding you towards the greatness that comes from living and loving the truth. It doesn't just keep you connected to what matters most but to what is **right**.

We must dig deeply to reconnect with the love beneath the lies.

9.
Tell me how unconditionally you love, respect and accept your partner/spouse, friends and family, knowing that they are your most important teachers.

If **the self-aware you** were telling me how unconditionally you love your partner, you might tell me that you start by getting to know your true self—and then unconditionally loving yourself, knowing that this allows others to fully know and love you.

You might tell me that allowing yourself to be truly seen and loved is another way of loving and expressing yourself. Likewise, you might tell me, not loving yourself is a way of rejecting your partner, since you are not fully committed to being all that you can be and are therefore rejecting parts of yourself—parts that are no more available to you than they are to them.

You might tell me that you understand the power of unconditional love—supporting your partner in being his or herself, without trying to get him or her to meet your needs.

You might tell me that resolving your own emotional neediness or insecurity (resulting from any early negative programming), and making yourself whole, is the biggest gift you could give yourself and others.

You might share with me your awareness of just how perfectly your partner triggers the issues from your past that are asking to be addressed, by reflecting what is going on inside you. You know that relating to your partner enables you to tell a new story about yourself, based on who you really are.

You might say you are grateful for all the teachers in your life and that, thanks to your own powerful magnetism, you always attract the lessons that you need in order to grow and become whole.

You might talk to me about the value of others in your life and how you can really only know yourself by actively relating to other people. Without them, you realize, you cannot know your strengths, your weaknesses, your inhibitions, your gifts, or your capacity for honest self-expression, love and compassion.

You cannot know how wise you are until you are called upon to share your wisdom with others.

You might tell me that you can see how others push you to grow, discover yourself and work your emotional 'muscles' by demonstrating the full range of healthy human emotions.

The truth leads to understanding,
understanding leads to acceptance,
acceptance leads to love,
and love unites us in our
mutual recognition of the truth.

10.
Tell me what's unique and special about you, what your heart yearns for and where that takes you.

You may not feel unique, yet we all have the capacity to be fabulous at something—in a unique way or in some particular aspect of life. Part of our purpose in life is finding that uniqueness and expressing it in ways that enrich us and others.

If *the quirky, creative, innovative you* were to share with me the many ways you might choose to express your uniqueness, you might tell me that you:

- sleep outside on the grass at least once a month;
- have a wickedly funny alter ego that only emerges when you write;
- make a habit of talking to animals and documenting your conversations;
- go to work on a pedal scooter;
- write the most profound poetry about ants;
- always ask deeply probing, mind-altering questions;
- can draw the faces of newborn babies as they will look when they're adults;
- wear your Hawaiian shirts at business meetings;
- can telepathically connect with close friends;
- inspire others to discover and share their innermost wisdom;
- make excellent organic wine from peppercorns, oranges and blackcurrants;
- instantly gain people's trust, inspiring them to tell you their deepest fears and secrets;

- make *papier mâché* sculptures from old novels;
- can heal physical pain just by thinking about it;
- make mattresses out of old flip-flops, tennis balls and chewing gum;
- create paintings that make people stare/laugh/cry/re-think their lives/find peace;
- can speed-read backwards;
- share laughter so infectious that people feel transformed;
- manifest what you desire within a week of envisioning it;
- contribute to your community and have heartfelt connections with everyone;
- take random walks in some new direction, with no map, phone or other props;
- live wildly, outside the box and inside your heart, inspiring the rebel in everyone you meet.

Or you might just tell me that you know you have a unique voice—a voice that no one else has or a voice that delivers a unique message.

If you were to tell me what your heart yearns for and where it takes you, you might say that you yearn for raw honesty and the courage to sustain it, knowing how powerfully it awakens the inner self.

You might tell me that you wish for the kind of spiritual connectedness that creates a tidal wave of compassion and empathy around the globe, dissolving anger, resentments and grief, while bathing everyone in the warmth of common understanding.

You might say you wish for a newfound awareness to pervade every powerful person, reminding them of their infinite capacity to live a superlative life.

You might share with me your desire for inspiration in your art, your words or your relationships, for the fulfillment of having touched even the most hardened or saddest of hearts.

You might tell me that you wish for peace where there was angst, for laughter where there was pain, for courage where there was fear, and for love where there was separation.

You might tell me that you yearn for every child to be free to grow unfettered by someone else's fears, to explore their own uniqueness, to discover their own wisdom and to keep their joyful innocence as they age.

You might tell me that your heart yearns for emotional walls to come down, for all pretence to dissolve, for all posturing to cease and for all interactions to be fuelled by kindness, honesty and truth.

You might tell me that you yearn for a return to real food and real medicine, to meaningful conversations and education, to integrity in politics and industry, to compassionate community and friendships, and to clean air, clean water and clean soil.

You might share with me your quest for purity—not just through the dissolution of cynicism and the revitalization of jaded hopes, but through the restoration of the pristine beauty of our natural world and the pure joy that comes from reconnecting with the genius and the magic fuelling every single human on earth.

You might tell me that all this takes you to a place of hope, of remembering what it means to be human and of knowing what lies deep inside each crippled soul, yearning to be cast free upon the world.

11.
Don't feed your story of who you are not. Share with me the simple joys of life and the purity of honest self-expression.

The true you might tell me that you know who you are not, which keeps you from allowing any pre-programmed imposters to run your life.

You are not your upbringing.

You are not your fears.

You are not your beliefs.

You are not your parents.

You are not your religion.

You are not your environment.

Most of all, you tell me, you are not other people's expectations or projections.

You are not a doormat to be walked on, a tender heart to be hurt into hiding, a lively spirit to be suppressed, a powerful presence to be contained, or an emerging hero to be told you must stay small.

You know the deeper truth.

If you were to share with me the simple joys of life, you would envelop me in laughter, you would touch me with your smile, you would grab my hand and run with me through the crunchy autumn leaves, you would look me in the eyes and tell me what you feel, you would stir me up with stories of the magic in your life, you would share with me your secrets, your goals, your passion and your joy.

You would hold a mirror to my soul by being your raw, authentic self and showing me how to be fully me.

12.
Don't give airtime to the lies passed on to you by those who did not understand the power of you. Tell me all the healthy ways you love, accept, respect and validate yourself.

If *the enlightened you* were to tell me all the ways you love, accept, respect and validate yourself, you might tell me that you first had to discover the truth about you. You had to dig deep to get beneath the layers of someone else's version of you, to find out who you really were, once you were free to truly be yourself.

You might tell me that you knew the way back home to you was by giving yourself those loving qualities not cultivated in you by others.

You might tell me that you go out of your way to embody love, acceptance, respect and validation for yourself—making healthy boundaries, saying no to whatever doesn't feel right to you, and putting yourself first in healthy, everyday ways.

You might tell me that you no longer make unhealthy compromises in the hope that others will like you. Now, you just want to like and know yourself. Since you have to live with you and you are the one you have to face in the stillness of the night when doubts or questions surface, you are the one who must be honoured and respected, above all others.

You know you must treat yourself as if you were your own best friend, always telling yourself the deepest possible truth and always standing up for yourself if challenged by others.

You might tell me that you recognize the purpose of others not understanding the power of you; in the absence of their awareness, you must find enlightenment inside, tapping into what feels profoundly true. In sensing that their perception of you feels limited (and recognizing that they also seem to be talking about themselves), you see that you are not them and that their projection is not you.

You realize that, in working to discover who you really are, you develop emotional and spiritual muscles you never knew you had.

In taking your more authentic self for a trial run with everyone you meet, you hear yourself speaking the truth and you like what you hear. You stand taller, you feel stronger, you go home feeling good about you—not because you are smug or vain, but because you are no longer betraying yourself by being someone you are not. You are letting go of the lies and you are honouring the real you.

You might tell me how good that feels and that you also see how it inspires others to be similarly honest and self-respecting.

If you were to tell me how you validate yourself, you might tell me that you have pushed through the lies that felt like the truth, dismantled the beliefs that seemed to form the scaffolding of your life, and done the most noble work of your life: giving your whole self back to you.

You might tell me that you have done what no one else could do for you yet what we must all do for ourselves.

You might tell me that you see the impact of setting the record straight—of reclaiming your true nature, catalysing change in others, and causing a subtle global shift because you are no longer making choices that work against you and that therefore work against the universe itself.

13.
Don't message me about how lonely and unconnected you feel.
Talk to me from the heart, up close and personal, expressing your deepest truth.
Tell me you remember how connected we already are.

If *the authentic you* were to express your deepest truth and to tell me you remember how connected we really are, you might tell me that it took a while. That you first had to experience being disconnected and to sense, in private moments of stillness, that some vital piece of the cosmic puzzle was missing.

You might tell me that feeling disconnected felt lonely, as if you were missing some lifelong friend who knew you like no other.

You might tell me that, even though you have many friends who love you, they are too distracted by life to see that something is missing—or that they distract themselves *because* they know that something important is missing.

If you were to tell me you remember how connected we already are, you might say that rediscovering that connection is like getting your heart plugged back into the universal grid. You feel energized and alert to the awareness of your interconnectedness, like the feeling of warm air on your skin on a sunny day where you cannot tell where your body ends and the air outside begins.

You might tell me that it required stillness and peace, that you had to separate yourself from the distractions and noise of life, to realize that the separation you felt was due to the separation from self.

In your busy world, your mind is always tethered by your thoughts, your soul in orbit without anchor, your heart often tightly boxed away.

Only in the stillness, you tell me, when you strip away the distractions, does your mind begin to expand, your soul resume residence and your heart begin to soften. Only then, you say, can you feel the connection that has always been there.

You might tell me that you feel an unfamiliar sense of power and a tingling of excitement at the enormity of your limitless self.

You might tell me that you feel connected to everyone and everything around you—as if all human hearts have suddenly opened, inviting you in without preamble or façade.

If you were to tell me how connected we already are, you might tell me with a loving look, a heartfelt hug, a listening presence and an openness that goes beyond mere words.

The truth is that we are all connected,
whether or not we feel connected
or want to be.

14.

Tell me about the compassion you feel— for your own pain, the pain of your fellow Earth-dwellers, the pain of the planet itself— and what you do with it.

As humans, we have the capacity to feel all kinds of pain— physical, emotional, mental and spiritual. We feel pain because we are designed to feel, yet we are not designed to feel pain for no purpose. Our pain is designed to take us somewhere, because it is the outcome of us having lost our way, of needing to go deeper within ourselves or of our hidden yearning to live a more expansive life.

We don't like pain, so we usually block it out. With more awareness, we may turn around and face it head on. If we can identify the emotional source of our pain, we can often take the action, say the words or take care of ourselves in the way that the body needs. Instead of getting angry at our body for causing us pain, we need to find compassion for it and for ourselves.

Our body is our most important messenger, and it makes no sense to attack it or reject it when it is trying to get us back on track with our healthy self.

If *the empathic you* were to tell me about the compassion you feel for your own pain, you might tell me that, if you are sick, unhappy or in pain, you always try to love, love, love your body as if your life depended on it …because it might.

You might tell me that your pain is not unique and that you know that others feel this same pain, even if they hide it.

You might tell me that hiding your pain is a way of pretending to be strong, even though embracing and healing our pain is a doorway to some greater strength and understanding.

If you were to tell me of the compassion you feel for others, you might tell me that you often feel their pain as if it were your own, and it helps you better understand the parts of them they have denied, as you have sometimes done. You might tell me that you strive to see the purpose of your pain so that pain does not become your life but your lifeline—a blessing in disguise to move you through whatever is keeping you stuck.

If you were to tell me of the compassion you feel for the planet itself, you might tell me that the polluting of the oceans is like pouring toxins into your bloodstream; that depleting natural resources is like working day and night without food or sleep; that emitting manmade radiation into the environment is like over-loading your body's delicate electrical circuits; and that forests being destroyed is like having your lungs filled with smoke.

You might tell me that your own pain is mirrored by the pain of the planet, and that healing your pain will also help to heal the wounds of our world.

Healing your emotional pain, you tell me, makes you profoundly aware of just how interdependent we are and how every choice you make can heal or steal from the earth.

The deeper truth dispels the lies
that keep us trapped
in a make-believe world
of struggle ad hardship.

15.
Don't talk to me about religion
or a vengeful god.
Tell me you remember that you *are* god,
creating your own lessons and
seeing the purpose of your pain.

Talking about spirituality does not come easily to many people. They are not comfortable with this aspect of themselves, if they are even aware that it exists. If people talk to them about it, they may not know what to say; if they talk about it to others, they may fear being considered flakey and not taken seriously.

If **the enlightened you** were to tell me about your spirituality, you might say that *not* talking about this vital aspect of you means that *you* are not taking yourself seriously.

You might tell me that you know this invisible part of you is the most powerful part.

You might say that, just as invisible radiation can often harm us more than what we can see, because we cannot see it, our spiritual essence has the power to do far more for us than the tangible, visible things in life ever can.

If you were to tell me about your faith in you and in the godness that surrounds you, you might tell me that faith in self is what makes your life work beautifully.

You might tell me that faith in self puts your power back where it belongs, inside you, rather than out there in some religious faith that hijacks your spirit, as if you need a go-between to plead your case for existing here on earth.

You might tell me that you have your own hotline to god—the god inside you and all around you.

You might tell me that depending on others for an interpretation of goodness and godness in the world robs you of your own spiritual autonomy.

You might say that nothing comes between you now and all your downloads come direct from source. You don't need a spiritual service-provider. You are your own satellite dish, picking up all the godness you need in the universe and freely going beyond your physical realm, where no earthbound religious intermediaries can ever take you.

The absence of love leaves our hearts empty, our souls unfulfilled and our destinies dwindling in the ethers.

16.
Tell me how you celebrate your spiritual essence and your limitless self.

If you were to tell me how you celebrate your spiritual essence, *the spiritual you* might say that it permeates everything you do, inspiring your choices, feeding your creativity and reminding you of the interconnectedness of everything.

You might tell me that your spirituality is your life force, fuelled by a soul that gets far too little airtime, given its crucial role in your life. You might say that you make time every day to meditate because it connects you with that subtle part of you that guides you towards your highest calling. Meditating creates stillness and peace inside, which allows answers to come to you when you are quiet enough to hear them. It's a time of inner wisdom making itself felt, when all the mental chattering eventually subsides and allows your whole self to be profoundly present.

You might share with me your realization that your soul is not a separate part of you or a component that you can set aside if you're too busy with other, more tangible things. The deeper truth, you say, is that you are your soul and your soul is you, taking you on your unique journey through life. Your soul serves to ignite your passion for being you and to unite you with your spiritual capacities for self-realization.

If you were to talk to me about your limitless self, you might say that the more you push your boundaries, going beyond the confines of conventional thinking, the more you see how limited a life you have led—and how limitless you really are.

You might tell me that you give thanks every day for your capacity to commune with universal intelligence and that you bask in the wonder of the unlimited possibilities that exist in your life.

17.
Don't tell me about your ideal life, with all the mod cons you could wish for.

Tell me that you understand the biggest con of all—the idea that our convenience matters more than our natural environment, our precious ecosystems and the planet that sustains us.

Tell me that you are choosing a higher path.

We all have different ideas of what constitutes an ideal life. Usually, we want life to be easy—easy money, easy work and easy relationships, with easy access to the food, services and amenities we need. But although life is meant to be easy, some kinds of easy make things hard for our planet. Filling our homes with gadgets, appliances and electronic devices takes a toll on our natural resources, in terms of the raw materials used to make those things or the energy required to recycle or dispose of them. Cars, motorized equipment and other fuel-dependent conveniences use precious finite resources that can never be replaced.

If **the mindful you** were to tell me that you understand the high cost of choosing convenience over the health of our planet, you might say that you can see the impact—not just in your environment but in those who live this way and how it changes them.

You might say that technology makes people less aware and less human, since they no longer use their hands or mental faculties to do or find things as before.

You might say that it disconnects them from the true source of all their possessions, in the same way that some children believe that their food comes from a supermarket rather than a farm.

You might tell me that people who don't actively care for the planet don't seem to take care of their bodies, either. Not because they really don't care but because they are so overwhelmed by the chaos or demands of their lives that they are disconnected. And if they are disconnected from their bodies, you tell me, they are unlikely to feel connected to Mother Earth. They must address the source of their chaos before they can tap into the source of their peace.

If you were to tell me that you were choosing a higher path, you might not say much at all. You might invite me to watch you living your life.

You might tell me that the higher path is inside you, invisible yet tangibly felt, guiding your decisions and your choices.

You might share with me how much more alive you feel. You might talk about the freedom you experience when you are not surrounded by inanimate gadgets that are designed to ultimately reduce the need for you in your own life.

You might say that you recognize the higher purpose of using the faculties that keep you balanced, dexterous and human.

The truth always connects you to your higher purpose.

18.

Tell me what passionate purpose lifts you out of bed each day and inspires you to live your life out loud.

Many things can propel us out of bed and into another day of choices and opportunities. It could be work, the need to take care of someone, hunger, habit, a sense of obligation or duty, or a need for action, to distract you from your worries. Some are propelled from their bed by some passionate quest or purpose. Having a passion for something energizes the whole body, generating ideas and the energy spurts needed to stay the course in the pursuit of some worthy goal.

If *the impassioned you* were to tell me what lifts you out of bed each day, inspired to live your life out loud, you might say that you love the work you do.

You might say you love your family and are deeply motivated to care for your children.

You might say that there is a book inside you that demands to be written and that you feel compelled and inspired to write it.

You might talk to me about some creative project that challenges your mind and ignites your imagination, lifting you out of your routine and bringing meaning and purpose to your days.

If you were to tell me what inspires you to live your life out loud, you might say that it is something that sets you apart—a unique skill, passion or view of the world that makes you feel alive and eager to make a difference.

You might say that it is simply an innate urge to create—to give birth to something extra-ordinary and to feel the power and fulfillment that come from realizing your wildest dreams.

19.

Don't tell me how smart your phone is
or how your car can drive itself.
Don't tell me about the identity microchip
embedded in your skin, opening doors
and bank accounts like magic.

Speak to me of *your* wisdom,
your own magical creatorship,
your awareness of the gift of life
and the power of your choices.

If you were to tell me of your wisdom, **the wise you** might say it was hard won—the result of digging deep inside yourself to find your own answers, of living an unconventional life because you somehow didn't fit in, and of sensing another layer of truth beneath the masks and façades of everyday life.

You might say that there are three levels of basic understanding that have taken you to a higher place, opening up a whole new world of possibilities and the realization that there are many more levels to attain.

The first level, you tell me, is like the kindergarten of life. This is when you act out all the negative programs from your upbringing, schooling, religion etc. You are unaware of what drives you and you develop all kinds of strategies to cope with life just 'happening'.

The second stage, you tell me, is like going to university, where you realize that there is a deeper truth to what's going on. You start to see what is driving your behaviour, your reactions, your circumstances and your choices. You begin to see how your negative beliefs distort and limit your perception of what's possible. You see that your life is a reflection of what you believe about yourself and you feel the conflict between the pull of your past and the pull towards a more enlightened future.

The third level, you tell me, is like going for training on another planet. This is when you start to remember who you really are and you begin to change your mind—to re-wire your brain, to dissolve negative neural networks, to consciously adopt new thoughts and emotions so you generate positive electromagnetism, to tap into your co-creative power, to engage your spiritual self, to reclaim your autonomy, and to feed your vision of your ultimate life so it becomes your new reality.

If you were to speak to me of your magical creatorship, you might tell me that you now understand that you are the creator of your own reality because you can tap into the vast interconnected web of energy in the universe—a universe of limitless possibilities.

You might tell me that you are striving to elevate your consciousness so that you can tap into these possibilities and draw them into your life.

You might tell me that you have seen how even placing your attention on something can change it.

If you were to speak to me of your awareness of the gift of life, you might tell me that you can see how brief and precious each life is, yet how tragically unaware most people are of their capacity for transformation.

You might tell me that, the more you connect with your spiritual self and with the consciousness of all other spirits out there, the more you realize that we are all one.

If you were to speak to me of the power of your choices, you might tell me that every choice you make has a consequence.

The love you express, the wounds you heal, the gifts you give and all your positive thoughts and heartfelt actions percolate throughout humanity, changing minds, opening hearts and awakening dormant souls.

You might tell me that your choices define you, telling the world what you think of you and what you think of it.

You might tell me that you know your choices have power because you know we are all connected, and that every choice you make now is a conscious one, fuelled by the awareness of its impact on your life and on your world.

Everyone has opinions.
But what you think of you
is all that matters
in creating your ideal life.

20.
Tell me what love and wonder you can instill with just your heart and hands.

With so much mechanization in our lives, we can sometimes disconnect from the magic in our hearts and hands.

If *the awakened you* were to tell me what love and wonder you can instill with just your heart and hands, you might tell me that you know your hands have power because you can physically feel it as a tingling life force.

You can feel the energy in the person whose hand you shake or whose body you hug.

You can feel the healing power of your hands when you place them on a loved one and visualize sending them your love through your fingers.

You might tell me that you know your hands are connected to your brain, your nervous system and every organ of your body. They are designed to detect, to sense, to feel, to create, to transmit subtle energies and to reach for what you want. They are designed to download your artistic visions onto the canvas, your inspired thinking onto the page, and your heartfelt emotions into the physical touch that reconnects you to your sensory self.

You might tell me that your hands are the servants of your heart, and your heart the puppeteer behind all your gestures.

You might tell me that you strive to keep your heart and hands open so that the full spectrum of human emotion can flow freely through them both, manifesting the fullness of life.

21.
Share with me the kindness, gifts and love that you have bestowed on others, enriching their life and yours.

Giving to others is the gift that we give ourselves. Acts of compassion and kindness touch our own hearts as much as those who receive them.

If **the compassionate you** were to tell me how giving to others has enriched your life and theirs, you might tell me that the act of giving and expressing your feelings puts you in touch with your heart, even if you initially did not feel like giving.

You might tell me that you know that giving to others keeps you feeling human and connected in some bigger way, beyond the petty concerns of everyday life.

You might tell me that just listening is a gift to those who need to pour our their hearts to someone who understands their pain.

You might tell me that you don't give to others so that you feel needed or loved; you give because unconditional giving is what heals us all. Unconditional giving means that you accept and love yourself enough to share it with others. In fact, you might tell me, such love just grows in the giving.

You might tell me that your life has been enriched by reaching out to someone homeless on the street, sitting down beside them to hear their story.

You might say you've been enriched by dropping a $50 note into the hat of a cash-strapped student busking on the pavement.

You might tell me that one of your most cherished memories is of visiting patients in palliative care, bringing them music, comic books, jokes and simple laughter.

You might tell me that all you needed to do was to silently hold someone's hand for you both to feel the love shared.

You might tell me that only by unconditionally giving can you open your heart to fully receive from others, and that only by fully allowing others to give to you can you know the healing power of unconditional acceptance in both directions.

Living and speaking the truth
is the greatest gift
we could ever give ourselves
or others.

22.

Don't tell me about the brave new wireless world; tell me how brave and resourceful *you* are in the face of loss, sickness, rejection, isolation and despair, using them as springboards for your growth.

We possess huge emotional and physical strength, yet we may feel weak and defeated in the face of some emotional or physical loss.

If *the empowered you* were to tell me how brave and resourceful you are in the face of loss, you might tell me that you don't just try to fill the hole created by it. You try to understand what that loss means, where it is trying to take you and why you might have needed this loss to awaken you to something buried deep inside.

You might tell me that loss can still bring you to your knees but that it can also bring you to your senses —to the expression of some deep grief, longing or old pain.

You might tell me that, when you get back up, you see things differently. You see how loss has given you a renewed awareness of the fleeting preciousness of life.

If you were to tell me how resourceful you are in the face of sickness, you might tell me that you know your body is talking to you. You know you haven't been listening properly and you know you must. You know that your body insists upon it, even as some deeper, wiser part of you reminds you that that is how things work. The body only brings you the messages that you failed to pick up because you didn't even think to check your body's inbox. You know you've been sending out lots of messages of your own, but not checking for feedback has thrown you off balance. You know you must clear your inbox and address your body's messages with as much focused presence as you can. Only then, you tell me, will you know what your body has been trying to tell you.

If you were to tell me how resourceful you are in the face of isolation, you might tell me that your isolation comes from insulation.

You might tell me that you see how you have insulated your heart against a deeper emotional connection—from feeling pain, from expressing a regret, from seeking forgiveness or from admitting to a weakness.

If you were to tell me how brave you are in the face of rejection, you might tell me that you know that being rejected by someone is merely an outward reflection of you having rejected yourself in some important way. You stand strong and you feel grateful for the mirrors and teachers you attract into your life so you can embody greater self-acceptance and then attract some shiny new mirrors of self-worth.

If you were to tell me how brave you are in the face of despair, you might tell me that you do not feel brave but that you know true courage means persisting in spite of being afraid.

You might tell me that your despair comes from having given up on yourself or from having temporarily lost faith in your capacity for greatness.

You might say that you sometimes look for reassurance of your value from others, yet you know that only you can restore your faith in you by doing something to impress yourself or by reconnecting with your spiritual self—the source of your greatness and the vast abiding presence that never lets you down. If you unplug from that universal bandwidth, you say, and allow yourself to believe that you are hopelessly alone, you know it's just your soul reminding you of how it feels to live inside that lie.

23.
Don't try to wow me with your gadgets; tell me how you embody eco-excellence on Earth.

Our 'smart' devices are captivating and seemingly miraculous in their mastery of so many functions. But they can pull us away from our own magnificence, keeping us focused on the evolution of *things* versus the evolution of hearts and minds.

If **the enlightened you** were to tell me how you embody eco-excellence on earth, you might tell me that you strive to stretch your mental muscles, to give your imagination a daily workout and to think creative thoughts without constraints.

You might tell me that you choose to operate outside the box—the box of toys, the box of modern housing, and the box that awaits you prematurely if you wither creatively and die before your time.

You might tell me that, for you, eco-excellence means using the very best in you—in healthy ways—to support the very best of nature on this earth.

You might tell me that this means finding ways to live an eco-friendly life—using water or recycled cooking oil to run your car, wearing clothing made from natural fabrics, choosing eco-friendly materials in your home, and reducing the demand for harmful wireless telecom systems while feeding the demand for healthier alternatives by supporting those creating them.

You might speak to me of your commitment to always choose the eco-friendly option—and that you always *do* have a choice. You might tell me that this choice is really not a choice at all but an imperative that underscores the most fundamental symbiosis of all: the planet's dependence on your integrity and your dependence on the physical integrity of your earthly home.

24.
Tell me that you still love nature—human nature and Mother Nature—and how you cherish both as doorways to the deeper truth.

Human nature and Mother Nature have all the best things in common—creativity, fertility, productivity, growth and a deeply spiritual essence. When human nature mirrors Mother Nature, we have balance. But if human nature defies it, denying its natural fragility or pretending it can meet our endless demands, the balance is lost and human dysfunction cuts deeply into the life force that sustains us.

If **the nature-loving you** were to tell me how you cherish human nature and Mother Nature as doorways to the deeper truth, you might say that there is no deeper truth than this: human nature is the doorway to consciousness and Mother Nature bears the evidence of our betrayal—betrayal of our own consciousness, of our capacity for greatness and of the planet that gives us the raw materials and the beauty for living an enchanted life.

You might share with me the ways you now strive to re-connect with nature, sitting in stillness in a peaceful forest clearing, or hiking up a steep mountain trail to gaze in wonder from the summit, experiencing nature's panoramic majesty while feeling the power of your own beating heart.

You might tell me that, up there, with nature spread out before you in a rich palette of colours, textures and life, you know that your pulse and the pulse of the earth are inextricably connected, with one depending absolutely on the other.

You might tell me that the true nature of our humanness is love and that, if you look around you, you will see that everything in nature is designed to love and nurture us—the oceans, oxygen, plant life, bountiful abundance, its music, its majestic beauty and its peace—and that all of those things are also designed to inspire love in us and for each other.

You might say that, as we deplete our planet's riches, we strip ourselves of the very things that inspire us to *stay* in love.

You might tell me that only consciously lived love will re-open the door to our hearts while closing the door on dysfunction.

Making choices based on our true nature supports our planet and our own health.

25.
Don't tell me how much money you have, what you do for a living, or how many friends you have on Facebook. Tell me what qualities define you as a human being and how you use them to elevate your existence.

In our materialistic world, our value is often measured in terms of how much money we have, the kind of home we own, the car we drive or the work we do. Those external things may make life more comfortable and easy, but they rarely bring us deep, abiding happiness or fulfillment. If we are largely humans doing rather than humans being, we may fail to find the inner contentment that comes from consciously cultivating our inner self.

Our material wealth will never give us a sense of healthy self-worth or self-acceptance, although we often try to find those qualities in external things. Yet those qualities are more about who we are than what we do.

If **the true you** were to tell me what qualities define you as a human being, you might tell me that your capacity for emotional honesty, empathy and compassion, and your ability to respond from the heart, are the qualities you most value and strive for. Your heart informs your head about what feels right so your head can make an inspired choice.

You might tell me that the qualities that define you are the ones you have consciously cultivated in yourself, rather than accepting others' ideas of who you should be.

You might tell me that you had to let go of the idea that you had to perform, impress, hide your shortcomings, compromise and be a fixer/care-taker in order to be liked and accepted.

You might say that recognizing the sense of obligation that many people feel when seeking acceptance tells you what is missing in them. And it is those missing qualities, you tell me, that are the most important of all. These are the things that people go to extreme lengths to obtain, even though they might appear to be striving for something else.

You might tell me that it's these invisible qualities—love, caring, respect and gratitude—that most define you as a human being and that most powerfully generate the good things in your life.

If you were to tell me how you use these qualities to upgrade your life, you might tell me that you simply drop the mask of pretension, letting go of any posturing, manipulation or contrivance designed to bring you what you want. Instead, you allow yourself to be seen, raw and self-accepting, for others to take or leave as they see fit.

You might tell me that dropping any neediness enables you to be happy on your own—and on your own terms—without the need for someone else to make you feel good about you.

You might tell me that your friends are few in number but that the quality of those friendships reflects your healthy self-worth, with no need for showy social displays.

You might tell me that those friends know you deeply, and you them, and that your conversations elevate you all, inspiring ideas and a deep appreciation for honest sharing.

You might tell me that little else matters, and that the heartfelt human connection trumps all other contenders in the quest for peace inside and out.

26.

Don't talk to me about electronic surveillance of your life.

Tell me how diligently *you* monitor your thoughts and words, your behaviour and boundaries.

Tell me that you are more healthily in charge of you than the other 'powers that be'.

There is much talk about all the data-gathering going on in our world, and many people resent these intrusions into their personal and professional life. With the growing invasiveness of Internet technology and with data being gathered about almost every aspect of our lives, it can sometimes feel as if there is nowhere to hide or be truly 'off the map'.

Being under constant surveillance may not feel nice. We value our privacy and don't like to feel exposed or manipulated by others.

If *the self-aware you* were to tell me how diligently *you* monitor your life, you might tell me that being monitored by others has prompted you to look much more closely at yourself.

You might tell me that the invasion of your privacy by commercially driven interests has inspired you to see just how well you know you.

You might tell me that you now consciously monitor your thoughts and words, your behaviour and boundaries, regaining control over you and those things that no one else can touch.

You monitor your words—not to censor them but because you know the power of what you say.

You monitor your thoughts because of the electrical charge they transmit, sending a message out into the world.

You monitor your emotions because they are magnetic, attracting more of the same.

You monitor your behaviour because it tells a story about you.

And you monitor your boundaries because where you draw the line tells people what you think you deserve.

You might tell me that, even though those 'powers that be' seek to influence your consumer choices and the information you can access, your awareness of their presence makes you even more aware of your own.

Being present, you tell me, enables you to make conscious choices based on what feels intuitively right for you. It enables you to let go of social pressures to fit in or buy the 'right stuff'.

You might tell me that looking closely at your own life also keeps you mindful of your lifestyle, attitude, reactions, relationship dynamics and the multitude of other things that have an impact on your sense of self, on others and on your environment.

You might say that conscious self-surveillance is a lifelong endeavour that enables you to track your progress as a human being (rather than a commodity), and as a unique individual striving to evolve on your own unique terms.

Truth is the only currency in life
that will never lose its value.

27.

Tell me when you feel the call to greatness and your connection to a higher realm.

A call to greatness can come to us in many different ways. It could be a wake-up call in the form of illness or a serious accident. It could be the loss of a loved one that leaves us facing our solitary self and pondering the point of our existence.

If *the spiritually aware you* were to tell me when you felt the call to greatness, you might say that the call had come in long ago but you ignored it, not wanting to answer it because you didn't think it was for you.

You might tell me that finally answering that call has engendered a whole new conversation with yourself.

You might tell me that the pivotal call came in the form of the loss of the life you knew. Stripped of your home, job, lifestyle and friends, you had only yourself to talk to.

You might tell me that you felt the call to greatness when you felt smaller than you ever had. You might tell me that this smallness felt so wrong that you knew you had to grow.

You might share with me how climbing back up to your full height and majesty required a potent fuelling from within.

You might tell me that the only comfort in your loneliness came from connecting to some higher realm. You might tell me that you hadn't known that it existed until you were pushed to find an answer to your pain.

You might tell me that now you feel the call to greatness every day and that you heed the call because it takes you where you were always meant to go.

28.

Tell me when you embrace your power to transform your world.

Tell me when you reclaim your rightful autonomy.

Tell me when I will hear about you on the good-news airwaves.

We have lost control over many important things—our food, medicine, health, governance and environment. This loss of control pushes us to reclaim responsibility for what matters to us in life. As industry and governments increasingly override our choices, we are challenged to reclaim our autonomy and to run our own lives.

If *the autonomous you* were to tell me when you reclaimed your power and your rightful autonomy, you might tell me that your body made you do it.

You might tell me that de-natured food, drug-based healthcare and environmental toxins pushed your body's tolerance past its limit.

You might tell me that your body gave you no choice—because *you* had not made healthy choices in its favour. To heal your body, you had to make new choices and to take back responsibility for your food, self-care and your home.

You might tell me that reclaiming your autonomy put you back in charge of you, fortifying your whole system and giving more meaning to your life.

If you were to tell me when I will hear about you on the good-news airwaves, you might encourage me to tune in to the cosmic channel, where all the news is good.

You might tell me to listen to my own intuitive guidance because the good news I hear about me will be the same good news you hear about you.

You might tell me that I will hear about you when I too start to transform my world and to connect with all the others doing the same.

The truth is that each one of us can make a difference because we are neurologically, spiritually, mentally, emotionally and physically designed to do so.

29.
Don't talk to me about
how much recycling you do;
tell me you no longer recycle your old
negative thoughts, patterns or projections.

Recycling plastic, paper and other packaging makes us feel as if we are doing something good for our planet. Yet it also prompts us to keep buying or using disposable materials, rather than breaking the cycle of recycling by using compostable or natural alternatives. The fact that precious natural resources are used to process or melt down plastics, paper etc is another reason why recycling is not necessarily an eco-friendly option.

If *the empowered you* were to talk to me about no longer recycling old emotional 'stuff', you might tell me that you have got your energy back.

You might tell me that, just as recycling disposable materials requires the use of precious non-renewable energy, recycling old negative beliefs was a drain on your whole system. Recycling negative thoughts and projections was also like a toxic cloud, hovering over you wherever you went.

You might say that refusing to recycle unhealthy patterns cleared the skies above you and freed you up to focus on more rewarding things.

You might say that you now control your thoughts, choosing those that serve you in creating what you want.

You might tell me that you catch yourself before you repeat old patterns, loving the difference that that makes in all your interactions.

You might tell me that your projections are now exclusively positive, promoting the positive outcomes that you seek.

You might tell me that no longer recycling old negative stuff means that you no longer waste your precious self on the past. Now, you propel yourself towards an enlightened future, while enjoying your own conscious presence in the moment.

No more dumping of toxic emotional waste into your personal environment, you tell me. Now you only recycle the positive new thoughts that promote the life you love.

Given our magnetism, we cannot afford to indulge in negativity.

30.
Don't tell me about
the faulty education system.

Tell me what you do to educate, enlighten and inspire yourself.

Tell me of your thirst for growth, self-awareness and universal wisdom.

As language breaks down under the pressures of texting in code, our communication skills suffer, as does our capacity to learn and to relate to others. The multi-tasking promoted by non-stop online connectivity fatigues the brain, affects memory and impairs our decision-making skills. As the pressures to perform continue to grow in an increasingly competitive world, education is often a matter of learning things by rote in order to 'make the grade'.

But true education is not about parroting someone else's knowledge; it's about learning to think for ourselves and to ask the kinds of questions that will expand our awareness of what's possible. It's also about being empowered to live our ideal life, whatever that might be.

If *the enlightened you* were to tell me what you do to educate yourself, you might tell me that you question everything and that you look for answers where few people go to find them.

You might tell me that you talk to plants, to young children and to the godness that you feel inside you.

You might tell me that you ponder the seemingly unknowable, asking yourself the kinds of questions that engage your imagination, with no need for answers ...although they sometimes come in unexpected ways.

Where in your body does laughter live?

What is love?

Why do limes never have pips, but lemons always do?

Where do your thoughts and feelings exist?

Why must you yawn if someone else does?

Must *we grow old and die?*

And where does the blue begin, up there in the sky?

You might tell me that the purpose of education is to expand your mind beyond what is already known, feeding your creativity so that you can contribute your unique perspective, insights or skills …or even just an original thought.

You might tell me that the flaws in our education systems can be seen in the torn fabric of society, showing us what we need to learn and what kind of life-affirming classes should be taught.

You might tell me that classes on civics or social studies should be replaced with classes on empowerment and self-mastery.

Classes on religious education should be replaced with classes on meditation and the power of the mind.

Learning about history should be replaced with learning about consciousness, self-awareness and how to be present rather than re-living the past.

Learning about creativity, quantum physics and how to manifest one's ideal life would serve us far more powerfully than home economics or chemistry.

With this kind of proactive cultivation of the human spirit, dedicated to the fullest evolution of every phenomenal being (you might tell me), we develop consciously, aware of our power, our creativity and our choices. We are no longer the result of random experiences determined by parental preferences, available schooling, whatever religion we are born into, or the beliefs passed on by those who failed to achieve their own potential or glimpse the deeper truth about life on earth.

You might tell me that you use these constraints to forge the true you—to excavate the essence of you buried beneath other people's projections.

If you were to tell me how you elevate yourself, you might say that you don't just feed your mind with books and other media. You seek to feed your emotional and spiritual selves, given their power to connect you with a deeper knowing.

You might tell me that you meditate every day to lift yourself out of the everyday to dance among the universal forces where all magic lives.

If you were to tell me how you enlighten and inspire yourself, you might say that you read books about human potential and watch documentaries on the plasticity of the brain and the power of the mind to bring light into your life.

You might say that your own creative writing inspires you to think and live more expansively, without any internal censors.

If you were to tell me of your thirst for growth, self-awareness and universal wisdom, you might tell me that they are all the same thing.

You might say:

What else is there, if not growth?

How can we be our true selves without self-awareness?

How can we attract like minds or the perfect partner if we are not showing up as our authentic selves?

And how one-dimensional would life be without the universal wisdom that inspires art, music, writing and innovation, beyond what we might consciously be able to create?

You might tell me that your thirst for growth is a thirst for evolution and fulfillment, for a deeper understanding of yourself and your place in the cosmos.

You might say that the wisdom you seek comes to you along the way, an integral part of the journey towards the destination that is you.

The truth is really all we have; everything else is drama and crisis designed to cover it up.

31.
Don't talk to me about the corruption of politicians and their inadequate policies.

Tell me about *your* policy for powerful living and all the ways you are living it.

Everyone has an opinion about whatever politicians are in power—and it's rarely positive.

If I were to ask you about *your* policy for powerful living, **the peaceful warrior** in you might tell me that your policy is simple: you strive for healthy self-governance—to operate yourself as fully as you can, mastering mind and body while harnessing all the skills that you possess.

You might tell me that no politician on earth can fix the problems of a nation, since those problems live inside each troubled person, distorting their perception of themselves so they rely on others to fix them or tell them what to do.

You might tell me that submissiveness promotes the loss of rights and entitlement so readily surrendered.

In every field of life, you tell me, there are too many sheep, too many wolves and not enough wise shepherds. The sheep wander aimlessly en masse, trusting in the safety of numbers and following each other around. The wolves are aggressive, moving in packs as they feast on the easy pickings, knowing they can overpower any of the helpless herds. The shepherds can see the problem but they are too few in number and too intimidated by the wolves to restore a healthy balance. They stand on the sidelines, devastated by the losses and vocal in their protests, yet they feel powerless to fight back.

You might tell me that you no longer live like a sheep; you have no desire to live like a wolf; and that becoming a good shepherd requires impeccable self-governance and a commitment to never relinquish your autonomy or the precious resources you have been gifted to protect.

If you were to talk to me of all the ways you live your policy for powerful living, you might tell me that you do not give away your power; rather than judging others or giving them airtime on your time, you strive to embody justice, fairness and integrity in all your interactions.

You might tell me that you honour your own values, with no need for regulation from outside.

You might say you are accountable to you, not to someone you voted into office to serve your needs.

You might tell me that you strive to meet your own needs so you avoid a life of political co-dependence.

You might tell me that whatever government is in power is a reflection of how empowered its citizens are in their own lives.

You might say that this shows you how you need to change so you can govern your own existence and win your own vote of confidence in you.

Corruption of the truth challenges us all to find our way back.

32.
Don't try to convince me that you are a victim of the system.

Tell me how you are being a leader in your own life.

Share with me the win–win victories you have forged.

Being a victim of a government, a company or a relationship is a clever way of opting out of self-determination. Victims cannot be victors, yet blaming others for one's problems seems to be a popular trend on earth. Victimhood fed by drama creates a never-ending cycle of self-defeating deception.

Since the dramas of life produced by our limiting beliefs confirm the validity of those beliefs, drama kings and drama queens can reign forever in their kingdoms of dysfunction.

If *the masterful maverick* in you were to tell me how you are being a leader in your own life, you might tell me that you gave up being a victim long ago.

You might say that you could see that it took more than it gave back and that victimhood removed you from the equation of your life.

You might tell me that courage + honesty + being your best self = inspiring leadership.

You might tell me that being a leader in your own life is the only way to orchestrate your life the way you wish.

You might say to me that true leadership comes from exploring and expressing all your skills and gifts, inspiring others to join you on your creative journey.

If you were to share with me the win–win victories you have forged, you might talk to me about the communities you have helped build; the 'disruptive thinking' workshops you have led; the young minds you have ignited; the creative projects you have promoted; the everyday activism you have inspired; the young entrepreneurs you have mentored; the partnerships you have cemented; and the lives you have transformed just by living yours so powerfully.

By leading in your own life,
you inspire others to lead in theirs.

33.
Don't speak to me of grudges or regrets.

Tell me you are learning to let go, and loving the freedom that it brings.

Holding on to negative feelings towards others corrodes our insides. We might feel envy, resentment or frustration, but whatever we feel is a reflection of an unmet need in us.

If we feel pain at not being respected, heard or treated kindly, it keeps us stuck in the past, subconsciously remembering some earlier time when we failed to get the respect, attention or kindness that we needed. We may conclude, deep down, that we don't deserve such things and then get angry or resentful if others re-open this old wound.

If **the forgiving you** were to speak to me of learning to let go, you might say that giving yourself what has been missing is the key to healing old resentments.

You might say that the best win—win solution is happiness as it sets you free to be yourself and to live in the present moment.

If you were to tell me how you love the freedom that this brings, you might say that a weight has been lifted off you, that you no longer focus on those grudges, that your energy is devoted to more rewarding things, and that you are truly happy to no longer be a reaction to someone else.

If you were to speak to me of letting go of regrets, you might say that who you were then is not who you are now.

You might say that being kind to yourself gives you the healthy self-acceptance that was missing in the past and that caused you to compromise—to not speak up, to not do what you wanted to do, to make your needs unimportant or to allow others to diminish you in some way.

You might say that it is only because you are wiser now that you can see how much more powerfully you could have lived, back then, had you known yourself better. If you did not have that higher wisdom now, you would not see your past choices as mistakes. Yet you know, too, that they were not mistakes since they took you to a place of greater self-awareness and compassion.

You might tell me that the more you let go, the more space you create for new things to come in.

You might tell me that letting go is not about letting others off the hook but about loving yourself. It is the conscious choice you make to wipe the slate clean and set yourself free to live your powerful life in the present.

The truth is the only springboard
and safety net that you will ever need.

34.
Don't dwell in darkness.
Show me how you shine your light
to cast away all shadows and self-doubt.

There is always darkness, at some point, somewhere in the world. And there is always some darkness inside us, at some point in our lives. Just as being unloved makes us yearn for love, being in the dark makes us yearn for light.

If I were to ask you how you shine your light to cast away all shadows and self-doubt, **the enlightened you** might tell me that your shadow is always with you, in sunshine and in rain, reminding you that you exist, that you have substance.

You might tell me that this silhouette of you changes all the time, depending on how much sun or shade is in your life.

You might tell me there are times when your shadow is strong, times when it stands beside you, and times when it is out of sight behind you.

You might tell me that you never try to lose your shadow because it tells you that you are in the light. If your shadow disappears completely, you say, you know you are in total darkness. But dwelling there, short term, has given you a long-term understanding. You know that dwelling there too long can make you wither, like a flower deprived of light. You know you need the light for you to be fully seen and for you to fully see others, and you strive to shine that light as often as you can.

If you were to tell me how you shine that light, you might say that you remember the power of the darkness and you do all that you can to return to the light—inside and out. You visualize light flowing into you from above, filling you up with warm energy. And you sit in the sunshine, feeling the warm rays of the sun on your face, relaxing muscles and bringing you a sense of peace.

If you were to tell me how you cast away self-doubt, you might say that you find words and images to lift your spirit, music to touch your heart, dynamic movement to dispel dark thoughts and laughter to eliminate stagnation.

You might tell me that your body holds old memories of darkness, programmed to keep you small or scared, but you remind yourself that you are bigger and brighter than any program you were taught.

You know that pushing back up into the light builds emotional muscles that keep your core strong. You know that choosing to shine rather than dwelling in darkness brings you the fulfillment you seek. You know that your commitment to not let the darkness win is an affirmation of your value as a being of light.

You might tell me that you help others to remember how much light they hold and how much they shine when they remember who they really are—and that this helps you remember your true self.

The darkness of dysfunction
cannot see itself.
Only conscious awareness reveals
the lies by which we live.

35.
Tell me how you master mind and spirit, tapping into universal intelligence to turn your life around. Tell me how you create your own heaven here on Earth.

If *the awakened you* were to share with me how you master mind and spirit, tapping into universal intelligence to turn your life around, you might tell me that you do this by:

- letting go of your past

- loving yourself for who you are

- embracing your spiritual essence

- staying in love with self, others and life

- reclaiming your personal autonomy

- allowing yourself to be powerful.

You might tell me that knowing yourself deeply is your lifelong quest, connecting you with your intuitive, spiritual and co-creative capacities.

You might say that you strive to live an impeccable life, catching yourself if you act without integrity and ensuring that your thoughts promote a healthy, happy you.

You might share with me your growing awareness of the innate intelligence that pervades all forms of life, bringing beauty, form and purpose to everything. You tap into this intelligence, you tell me, by meditating in stillness, allowing the deeper parts of you to connect with the consciousness that connects all things.

If you were to speak to me about creating your own heaven here on earth, you might tell me that being uncompromisingly you is the answer.

Heaven, you might say, is loving your life and having life love you back. When you are thrilled to be you and in awe of your creative capacities, each day brings wonder and joy as you embrace your potential and leverage the magic of the universe, forever expanding your vision of what's possible.

Pre-living and pre-loving your ideal life makes it come true in your world.

36.
Tell me the truth about you.

The truth about you is good news. In fact, it is nothing *but* good news.

If **the real you** were to tell me the truth about you, you might say that the truth about you is the truth about me.

You might say that you can see yourself in me and me in you. You might say that I am you because of the many aspects of you that I have met along the way—the you that challenged me, encouraged me, judged me, rejected me, loved me and mirrored me. I am who I am because I either reacted to you, cementing my programming, or I responded differently, growing beyond the smaller me that I used to be.

You might say that you, in all your many guises, enabled me to let go of my multiple disguises.

If you were to tell me the truth about you, you would say that you know how it feels to live the deeper truth of who you are because everything works. Life is easy. Love abounds. Friendships blossom. Money flows. Business, career and creative projects succeed in win–win ways.

You are always in the right place at the right time, in tune with the flow of the universe and your own inner guidance.

You might tell me that the more you live this life, the more you live this life …and the more you love it.

You might tell me that when you live this way, you fall in love with everything and everything loves you back.

37.
Tell me what I would love about you
if I met you.

If you were to tell me what I would love about you if I met you, **the wise you** might say that I would love the real you if I really knew you ...and if you allowed me to see the real you.

You might say that I am you and you are me and we are constantly merging and re-emerging.

You might say that, with deep understanding comes acceptance, and with unconditional acceptance comes love.

You might tell me that you would love me for being authentic, vulnerable and emotionally honest.

You might tell me that you would love me being me and that that is the only truth you would ever want, now that you know the power of me being who I really am.

The truth is the ultimate reality
and nothing less than that will do,
once you know the truth about you.

38.
Tell me who you are
and why you are proud to be you.

If **the honest you** were to tell me why you are proud to be you, you might say that you are proud of not having lived a life of mediocrity or submissiveness.

You are proud to have rejected convention in favour of your dedication to the truth and to your uniqueness.

You are proud of not succumbing to the pre-programmed limitations that could have kept you small forever, had you not chosen to expand your vision of yourself.

You might tell me that uncovering your true self is the most challenging but most noble and rewarding thing you have ever done.

You might tell me that your efforts to know yourself fully have enriched your experience of life, giving you a unique perspective of your power, your place and your purpose in the universal scheme of things.

You might tell me that you are proud of having come home to you, on your own terms and in your own unique way.

The truth will always guide you home.

39.
Tell me why you are here
and why I will miss you when you are gone.

If *the enlightened you* were to tell me why I might miss you when you are gone, you might say that there are two kinds of missing.

You can miss a person even when they are alive, if they fail to fulfill their potential to become the person they were meant to be. You can miss the parts of them that you know are buried deep inside, not daring to come out, and that go with them to their grave without ever being expressed. You can miss that kind of person because of what was missing in their lives and what you missed sharing with them; you can miss not having had a deeper connection, the love or the meaningful exchanges that you would have loved to have with them.

You might tell me that this kind of missing carries a double sadness—for the loss of the person in your life and for their lack of personal fulfillment. This kind of missing holds regrets and leaves a hole where the missing person used to be.

The second kind of missing can also cause sadness, but it is tempered by rich memories of a life fully lived. You can miss a person when they are gone yet carry their positive presence with you if they strove to be all that they could be.

You might tell me that I will miss you most if you fail to be yourself while you are here, leaving a gaping hole that no one else can ever fill.

40.
Tell me the truth, the whole truth
and nothing but the truth
...and we will all be free.

The truth is all we've got left. We've tried everything else.

We've tried wars, terror and torture.
We've tried prisons, punishment and blame.
We've tried religion, judgement and damnation.
We've tried lies, corruption, manipulation and deceit.
...and we have not found freedom.

We've tried indulgence, gadgets and distractions.
We've tried exploitation, addiction and depravity.
We've tried violence, violation and shame.
We've tried disease, self-rejection and subservience.
...and we are still not free.

We've sold our souls and hijacked our hearts.
We've plundered our planet and irradiated the globe
leaving us with nowhere else to go.
...and we have never been so far from free.

We've tried everything on earth to hide
from our dysfunction and denial.

We are oblivious to the consciousness that connects us
with a universe of mind-blowing possibilities.

We've tried everything outside of us,
while denying the magic within.

The deeper truth of our self-mastery is the one thing
we have not collectively cultivated in our lives,
yet it is the key to freedom and fulfillment.

Tell me the truth, the whole truth and nothing but the truth
...and then live it.

This is our higher calling. It is our only way back.

There is nothing else left for us to do.

We are born open, without prejudice, malice or preconceived ideas. We are pure, with a clean slate, an open heart and a fresh mind like a sponge for absorbing life. We are born free, unfettered and multi-faceted, endowed with all the skills, creativity and faculties we could possibly need for a life of joyous exploration, self-discovery and fulfillment. As babies, we are the essence of **freedom**, without constraints on our needs or desires, our feelings or our bodily functions. We are perfect, simple and spontaneous. We have awareness so we can measure our progress and evolution. Our driving impetus **is** to experience, to feel, to express, to love and to be our unique self. We are uncomplicated, devoid of lies or subterfuge. Being our authentic selves is **our** birthright and our greatest responsibility. We exist as individuals to experience our own uniqueness and to reconnect with the **natural** oneness of our collective humanity. Our physicality is protected within a skin but it does not contain us. We are designed to join in wonder and joy, without conflict, confusion, separation or strife, uniting in a mindful **state** of tender connectedness. We are spiritual beings, in a miraculously intricate body, with billions of cells responding and regenerating, with neurons firing, networking and manifesting, a universe unto itself, existing within a limitless cosmos that responds to our cues, thoughts, emotions and intent— our magnets for magnificence—giving us the power to create whatever scenarios we choose, to learn, grow, understand and evolve, elevating our existence as we connect with our own consciousness and with universal intelligence inside and out. We are born childlike yet godlike, filled with playful, creative godness and goodness, eager to embody both in every conceivable way, reaching heights of excellence and unimagined mastery in living the magical truth of who we really are.

About the author

Olga Sheean is a writer, educator, relationship counsellor and empowerment coach specializing in human dynamics and quantum potential. An 'archaeologist of the mind', she is dedicated to excavating the deeper truth buried in every complex, amazing, powerful human being. Using her own unique framework for self-mastery, she helps people transform the negative subconscious programs that drive their circumstances, relationships, self-worth and success.

Olga has worked as a photojournalist for the World Wide Fund for Nature (WWF) International in Switzerland and as an editor for the United Nations in Geneva. A former magazine editor and health columnist, she is a prolific writer who has published over 300 articles in various magazines and regularly feeds her two blogs: *The O Zone—a place of positive e-missions* and *Beyond Belief—exposing the deeper truth*.

In her downtime, Olga does kundalini yoga, plays 'silly Scrabble' (inventing new words), bounces on her 14-foot trampoline, enjoys reckless, rule-free table tennis, and reads voraciously.

She is the author of five other books:

- *Fit for Love: find your self and your perfect mate*

- *Gut Feelings—the inside story*

- *The Alphabet of Powerful Existence: an A–Z guide to well-being, wisdom and worthiness*

- *A Talk on the Wild Side—imaginary interviews with unlikely sources of wisdom*

- *EMF off!—a call to consciousness in our misguidedly microwaved world*

All her books are available at https://olgasheean.com/books.

For more info or to contact Olga, please see her empowerment website (https://olgasheean.com), where you can read about relationships and empowered, holistic living, access her blogs, purchase her books and recorded affirmations, and sign up for her newsletter.

You can download her free documents on electromagnetic radiation from her EMF website, which has further details about *EMF off!—a call to consciousness in our misguidedly microwaved world*, as well as a blog, additional resources and information about electromagnetic radiation: https://emfoff.com.